Julian

Be encouraged!

Shelm
& Roy

9 Fundamentals of **Golf** That Will Change Your Life

Transform Your Game

ROGER and BECKY TIRABASSI

HOWARD

ABOUT THE AUTHORS

Roger Tirabassi is a certified sports counselor as well as a licensed professional counselor who regularly helps clients adjust and improve their weaknesses in life.

Becky Tirabassi is a certified life coach, motivational speaker and the founder of Becky Tirabassi Change Your Life ®, Inc., a multimedia company that encourages people to improve or transform their lives for the better through Change Your Life ® resources, events, and media presentations.

Rick Hunter is a PGA Instructor and Member.

Roger, Becky, and Rick are also the co-authors of *The Front Nine: Nine Fundamentals of Golf That Will Improve Your Marriage.*

To contact

Becky Tirabassi and/or Roger Tirabassi please call, e-mail, or write them at:

1-800-444-6189

www.transformyourgame.com

becky@transformyourgame.com

Change Your Life, Inc.

Box 9672

Newport Beach, CA 92660

Transform Your Game © 2004 by Roger and Becky Tirabassi

Published by Howard Publishing Co., Inc.
3117 North 7th Street, West Monroe, Louisiana 71291-2227
www.howardpublishing.com

04 05 06 07 08 09 10 11 12 13   10 9 8 7 6 5 4 3 2 1

Edited by Between the Lines
Cover and interior design by LinDee Loveland and Stephanie D. Walker
Photography by LinDee Loveland and Chrys Howard

Special thanks to:
Tustin Ranch Golf Club, 12442 Tustin Ranch Road, Tustin, California 92782
Callaway Golf Company, 2180 Rutherford Road, Carlsbad, California 92008
Rick Hunter, PGA Instructor, Impact Golf Swing Systems and Training Aids
RHunterRAH@aol.com

ISBN: 1-58229-373-2

Contents

INTRODUCTION

Observers of the game of golf often think it looks fun and easy—until they pick up a club and try hitting a ball. Beginning players quickly learn that golf is a complex sport that engages all of one's faculties—body, mind, and emotion.

Serious golfers are rarely content with their game. Whether it's a change in grip, stance, swing, equipment, follow-through, or even their mental state, one thing is sure: golf is a game of continuous transformation made up of a number of fundamentals that, when mastered, result in greater satisfaction and a better game.

As a family who golfs together, we fell into a pattern of golfing every Sunday afternoon. We meet up with Becky's brother, Rick, and their eighty-two-year-old mother. We all come with varying levels of

1

skill, but the handicap system allows for plenty of friendly, if some-times feisty, competition at our weekly outing.

The Golf Channel once interviewed us, and under Becky's name, their caption read "Much more competitive than Roger."

This competitive attitude apparently runs in the family. Becky's mom (who plays four times a week) is just as busy on Sundays trying to beat Becky. And of course, everyone wants to beat Rick (the PGA member) on at least one hole each round.

Golf has taught us much about our competitive spirits, but our greatest discovery is that the fundamentals of golf that will improve our game also easily and effectively translate into principles that can change our lives.

As a PGA instructor, Rick meets men and women every day who want to change or improve some aspect of their golf game.

In our fields as a professional counselor (Roger) and motivational speaker (Becky), we constantly encounter people who deeply desire to change one or more areas of their lives. When asked what they would improve, they often list marriage, fitness level, relationships, finances, or professional status. Many people share unfulfilled dreams or long-term goals that seem unreachable.

Whatever your dream or goal is, we're convinced that applying the fundamentals in this book can help you realize greater fulfill-ment, achievement, and reward—both in your game and in your life.

For example, as a pre-shot routine in golf builds confidence under pressure, so incorporating new habits into the daily disciplines of your life may be the catalyst you need to move to a new level of personal or professional accomplishment. Or the "Stay Calm, Play Calm" fundamental might give you new insight on how uncontrolled emotions have a negative affect on everyone's day, including yours.

In *Transform Your Game*, we'll take nine golf fundamentals and pose the question, How will this fundamental take me to a new level of personal and professional performance, achievement, or transformation?

The purpose of *Transform Your Game* is to inspire you to incorporate the proven fundamentals of golf into every area of your life and allow them to enhance your performance—at work, at home, and especially on the course!

Our hope is that each chapter will . . .

- Increase your enjoyment, understanding, and performance of the game of golf.
- Provide an ideal training ground for self-improvement by giving you examples from golf that translate into teaching tools for life.
- Show you how to take your personal and professional goals to the next level by giving you practical examples for better communication, self-control, and goal setting.

We love golf, but we're even more passionate about equipping people to reach their potential and positively transform their lives. Whether you picked up *Transform Your Game* to improve your game or change your life, we're convinced these fundamentals will help you do both!

Begin with a Charge

THERE IS NO TYPE OF MIRACLE
THAT CANNOT HAPPEN AT LEAST ONCE IN GOLF.

Grantland Rice

5

FUNDAMENTAL #1

BEGIN WITH A CHARGE

Golf's most exciting moments revolve around the comeback of an underdog or the rally of a favorite player who climbs from behind the pack, scratching, clawing, and brilliantly playing to the top of the leader board.

In these moments you can feel the excitement and momentum rumbling down the fairways and filling the gallery of spectators. It's clear that something great is about to happen, and it almost always comes down to the last round, last hole, or last putt. It's what makes golf so dramatic, so great, and so passionate.

The U.S. Open is one golf tournament that regularly delivers thrilling suspense and great comebacks.

In 1960, before Sunday's final round in the U.S. Open, several

7

reporters were discussing the tournament over lunch. They all agreed that Arnold Palmer, who was fifteen places back and had never won the Open, didn't have a chance. But Palmer overheard the men and goaded them with a watch-and-see challenge.

Palmer began his charge with the first tee shot. He blasted it to the edge of the green and birdied the first hole. And he didn't stop there. Palmer impressively birdied holes two, three, four, six, and seven. His only bogey came on number eight, where he fired up the crowd by two-putting out of a sand trap. His front-nine round of thirty set the U.S. Open record. He finished up the back nine with one more birdie for a final round of sixty-five.

Against all odds, Palmer overtook a field of legends that included Jack Nicklaus and Ben Hogan to win his *only* U.S. Open title.

No one was more surprised than the reporters who had doubted he could come from so far behind to win. By the end of the day, they were summing up Palmer's great determination and flawless performance with just one word: *charge!* His victory is considered one of the greatest come-from-behind wins in the history of the tournament.

Avid fans watch touring professionals play golf for hours, because they know the momentum can turn at any time. Commentators often can pinpoint the very hole when the tournament shifts, and a player passionately clinches a spectacular victory.

Whether you're a professional or amateur golfer, in every round of golf, there comes a moment when you must begin a *charge*—to intentionally make a move.

9

IN EVERY ROUND OF GOLF, THERE COMES A

MOMENT WHEN YOU MUST BEGIN A

CHARGE—TO INTENTIONALLY MAKE A MOVE.

Sometimes the charge is called for at the outset of the game. The first shot sails out of bounds, and the round starts with a penalty. Do you let disappointment drown out your enthusiasm, or do you take your penalty and vow to make it up immediately with a great next shot?

Or somewhere in the middle of the round, a few putts rim the cup instead of dropping—do you let disappointment turn into frustration, or do you simply focus on the next shot?

Sometimes a charge must be mounted at the end of the round. Perhaps your best round ever is unfolding, and on the eighteenth hole, you hit a beautiful drive but get a bad bounce. Do you get upset and distracted, or do you quickly harness your emotions and finish strong?

A charge begins with a thought, a choice, or a shot that suddenly and dramatically shifts your momentum. A charge is a decision—it doesn't just happen. It's the point when you *choose to pursue victory* with purpose and passion, no matter what lies behind.

BEGIN WITH A CHARGE

Change means turning around.

By the time Becky was twenty-one, her personal and legal troubles were out of control due to a lifestyle filled with drugs and alcohol. Events culminated one morning at a court hearing, and afterward she finally admitted she was an addict.

There was no question in Becky's mind that something had to change. Yet she didn't believe she was strong enough to overcome her addictions. Suicide seemed the only way out.

But a serendipitous series of events unfolded that same morning that led to a dramatic turnaround—a change of friends, thinking, and behavior.

It began with one decision—to turn.

Becky vowed to stop using drugs and alcohol, and she started living. She asked for help. Becky's charge to change began immediately. She went from suicidal to peaceful, addicted to sober, and began a whole new life.

When we're faced with the challenge of achieving a goal or making a difficult change in our lives, that challenge requires many things; but the first step is acknowledging that the time has come to live, work, or love differently. We must make a decision, even say the words aloud to others and to ourselves, "It's time to change *now*. I've got to begin this today."

Whether starting over because of a setback or venturing into unknown territory, we often face incredible odds and a head full of discouraging thoughts that try to stop us before we get started.

Change in your life begins with a charge—an attitude that releases power, hope, enthusiasm, and determination.

In Becky's book *Change Your Life*, she lays out four steps or stages of change: (1) Change begins with *awareness*. (2) It is empowered by

"It's time to change *now*. I've got to begin this today."

admission, (3) achieved through a written daily *action plan*, and (4) sustained with *accountability*.

Begin by identifying your challenge—whether you need to lose twenty-five pounds, start a new career, or restore a broken relationship. What do you want or need to change or improve?

Dwell on positive thoughts that revive your spirit, fill you with hope, and fuel your courage to get back up and start again.

You might include some thoughts like these:

- It's never too late to change.
- I can do this.
- There is hope.
- Forget the past; look ahead.
- There is no better time than right now.
- There's help if I need it.
- Don't be afraid.

Though change is a process, it has a beginning. If you're ready and willing, even begging for breakthrough or success in your life, begin the charge right now!

*The most significant common intangible among the truly great
is that they enjoy adversity.*

GARY PLAYER

EVERY DAY YOU DON'T HIT BALLS IS ONE DAY LONGER
IT TAKES YOU TO GET BETTER.

Ben Hogan

FUNDAMENTAL #2

Practice like the Pros

FUNDAMENTAL #2

PRACTICE LIKE THE PROS

Perhaps the real difference between amateur and professional golfers is that pros know—through experience—that there are no short cuts to becoming a great golfer.

In *The Golfer's Guide to the Meaning of Life*, world-renowned golfer Gary Player tells of the practice regimen he used as a young man that included "practicing and hitting as many balls as is humanly possible." He recalls his "fascination with how hard Arnold Palmer practiced." And when Player refers to Tiger Woods, he does so with admiration and respect: "Tiger has loads of talent, but the thing that makes him a champion is that he outworks every other player in the game. He practices harder and smarter and longer than all the rest."

What should the average golfer focus on during practice sessions?

18

PRACTICING ANYTHING CAN

SEEM LIKE DRUDGERY BECAUSE

IT REQUIRES TIME AND DISCIPLINE.

One of the premiere golf instructors of the twentieth century, Harvey Penick, believed that practicing in the area of your weakness is the way to improve your game. "The irony," he said, "is that people prefer to practice their strengths."

Penick recommended: "For two weeks devote 90 percent of your practice time to chipping and putting, and only 10 percent to the full swing. If you do this, your 95 will turn into 90. I guarantee it."

This sounds easy. But practicing *anything* can seem like drudgery because it requires time and discipline.

Tom Watson suggests, "The most valuable time to practice is right after your round, when your mistakes are fresh in your mind." Amazingly, after long hours of tournament play, you'll find many of the pros on the practice range until dark.

Practice—and lots of it—is simply not an option for players who want to lower their handicap or take their game to the next level.

PRACTICE LIKE THE PROS

If you are pursuing a change in lifestyle or a career advancement, learning from experts in that field doesn't always take money—but it will take time. Too often, when we don't see immediate results from

What separates the best from the merely talented is a continuing passion to learn more and get better.

study or practice, we procrastinate, prepare haphazardly, wing it, or just ditch it.

Most successful people choose their field because they have natural talent in that area. But what separates the best from the merely talented is a continuing passion to learn more and get better. You'll find these high achievers reading and attending seminars to increase understanding and to improve or learn some skill. They exhibit extra effort in their professions, pleasures, and personal lives.

In Roger's counseling practice, he frequently asks clients, "Are you willing to do whatever is necessary to make this change?" Initially, most people eagerly say, "Oh yes. I'll do whatever it takes!" But when he presents them with tangible, practical steps for improvement (like displaying rigorous honesty, reading relevant literature, getting an accountability partner, giving up the right to play the victim, or turning over their will to God), the eagerness tends to fade and the excuses begin.

Changing your life, reaching a goal, or making adjustments requires sacrifices. It takes time, commitment, and independence. But if you're serious about making progress, you'll make the extra effort.

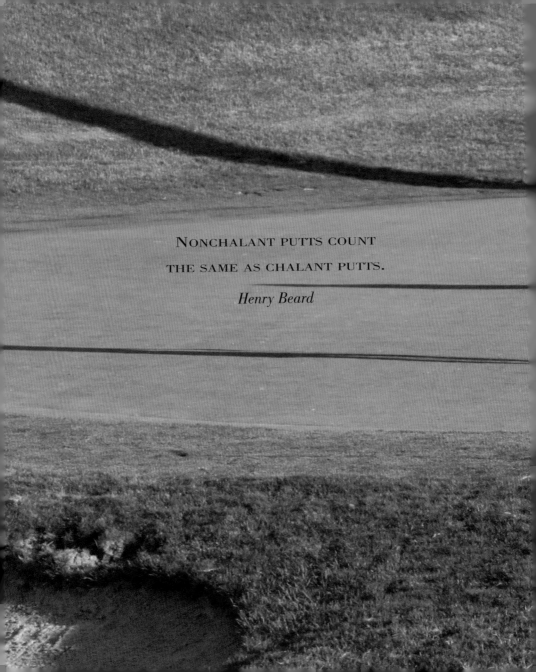

NONCHALANT PUTTS COUNT
THE SAME AS CHALANT PUTTS.

Henry Beard

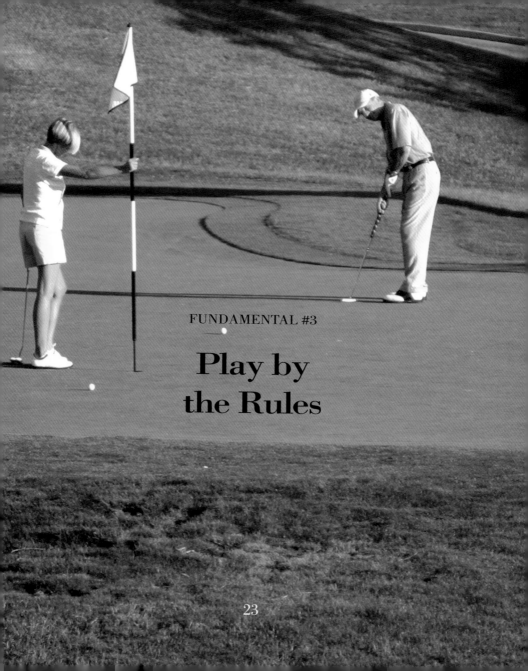

FUNDAMENTAL #3

Play by
the Rules

FUNDAMENTAL #3

PLAY BY THE RULES

Becky played the game of golf on and off for years but only became serious about it a few years ago. While seated in a waiting area of an airport, she was enthusiastically highlighting and underlining in *Harvey Penick's Little Red Book*. A woman next to her asked, "Are you a golfer?"

Becky replied proudly, "Oh, yes!"

Little did Becky realize this conversation would become a defining moment, leading her to take her golf game to the next level.

"What's your handicap?" the woman inquired.

Becky felt a bit embarrassed because she played regularly but didn't have a handicap. "I don't really have one," she admitted.

YOU'LL NEVER KNOW IF YOUR GAME IS

IMPROVING IF YOU AREN'T RECORDING

YOUR ACTUAL SCORES.

The woman was blunt and to the point: "Well, without a handicap, you're not really a golfer. You can't play in a league or competition without a handicap. And you'll never know if your game is improving if you aren't recording your actual scores."

Before Becky found out that this woman had a two handicap, she asked naively, "How do you get a handicap?"

"You have to record an attested score for twenty rounds of eighteen holes playing by the USGA rules. You're required to count any whiffs and out-of-bounds penalties, and you can only improve your lie when the rules allow you to do so." She added matter-of-factly, "You have to play by the rules if you want to be taken seriously as a golfer."

The next spring Becky enrolled in a local golf association and began golfing as often as possible—not just nine but eighteen holes—counting every shot and playing by the rules. By that summer she had a handicap. No more gimmes; no more mulligans. Counting a few whiffs along the way, she continually sets goals to lower her handicap.

Golf has so many rules that most players carry a USGA rule book in their bag as a reference to ensure accuracy. Even on tour, officials are available to advise professionals of the official rule for their situation, and players help police the round for each other, acutely aware that not following the rules can result in disqualification.

The game requires a level of integrity that begins with a decision before teeing off: *I will follow the rules.*

- I will count all strokes—including whiffs.
- I will take the penalties for balls that go out of bounds.

- I will play my ball where I find it, not improving a bad lie unless allowed by the rules.
- I will putt out on every green, not taking gimmes.
- I will not take any mulligans.

Jack Nicklaus candidly admits what all serious golfers understand: "If there's one thing golf demands above all else, it's honesty."

Playing by the rules of golf is a decision. If you choose to play by them, you—and others—will take your game more seriously, and you'll inevitably become a better player.

PLAY BY THE RULES

The rules of life—honesty, faithfulness, kindness, compassion, and generosity—have the ability to make you a better person *if* you decide to live by them.

For example . . .

- Faithfulness in a marriage builds trust.
- Honesty on a tax return builds integrity.
- Fairness toward coworkers builds a good reputation.

When you find yourself confronted by the rules of life . . . remember that everything hinges on whether you decide to play by them.

- Following the rules of life will help you develop strong character, improve self-esteem, and gain the respect of others. It also can protect us from humiliation.

But our adherence to the rules is tested most when no one is looking.

Roger frequently sees clients who want to improve their relationships, overcome addiction, or achieve a specific fitness or financial goal, but they just can't seem to find lasting change.

It isn't because they don't *know* the rules. They just haven't made a decision to live by them.

For example, most people know the rules of marriage: It takes two people who are completely committed to effective communication, flexibility, sacrifice, and love to maintain a healthy marriage. But if both parties aren't going to play by the same rules, especially when no one is watching, the inconsistencies can create a breaking point.

There are rules for people who struggle with addiction too. The first one is abstinence. If you try to fudge on the rule and allow exceptions here and there, "here and there" has a sneaky way of causing relapse.

When you find yourself confronted by the rules of life—whether by inspiration or desperation—remember that everything hinges on whether you decide to play by them. Winning the game of life means being honest about who you are, what you've done, how your actions impact others, and what success really requires.

It also means owning up to penalties when you deserve them. You know when a comment, action, or thought is out of line. Call yourself on it and admit your mistakes to others.

If you want to see real change, growth, and achievement in your life, commit to following the rules even—and especially—when no one is watching.

The man who can go into a patch of rough alone, with the knowledge that only God is watching him, and play his ball where it lies is the man who will serve you faithfully and well.

P. G. WODEHOUSE

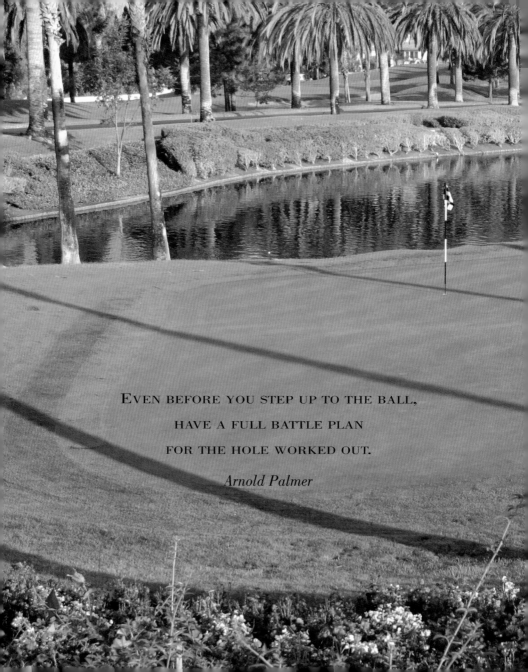

EVEN BEFORE YOU STEP UP TO THE BALL,

HAVE A FULL BATTLE PLAN

FOR THE HOLE WORKED OUT.

Arnold Palmer

FUNDAMENTAL #4

Develop a Green-to-Tee Strategy

FUNDAMENTAL #4

DEVELOP A GREEN-TO-TEE STRATEGY

Tour players take course management very seriously. Before a tournament it's not unusual for competitors to play the course—sometimes more than once. Without the pressure of competition, they can assess any areas of difficulty, determine the speed of the greens, and practice a variety of shots. Come game day, the best players have developed a green-to-tee strategy.

The process begins with mentally playing each hole in reverse, the competitors imagining themselves standing at the back of the green. They observe the pin placement and determine the direction from which they want the ball to enter the hole. Next they decide the best approach shot to get the ball to the desired position. Now they have a target for their tee shot.

36

WORKING OUT A STRATEGY WILL GIVE

YOU MORE CONFIDENCE DURING THE

HEAT OF COMPETITION.

No matter your skill level, working out a strategy—in advance—will give you more confidence during the heat of competition, keep you from making impulsive shots, and give you a tangible plan for reaching your scoring goals.

DEVELOP A GREEN-TO-TEE STRATEGY

In life, course management translates into setting goals and developing a strategy to reach those goals.

To change your life radically and permanently, you must set goals that are broken down into daily strategies. Equally important is a willingness to hang in there for the long haul. In his work with champion golfers, psychologist Bob Rotella says the defining characteristics of any champion—not just golfers—are that "they are all strong-willed, they all have their dreams, and they all make a long-term commitment to pursue those dreams."

Aha! The key to fulfilling long-term dreams or achieving a big goal is not a secret. It hinges on having a plan—and the will—to succeed.

If you want to achieve change or fulfill a dream, begin by writing down your goals.

Having struggled with alcoholism and anger, she knows the difficulty of overcoming character flaws.

A legendary study conducted by Harvard University asked MBA graduates, "Have you set clear, written goals for your future and made plans to accomplish them?"

Upon graduating, only 3 percent of the students had put specific goals and plans in writing. Thirteen percent said they had goals but hadn't written them down. Eighty-four percent responded that they had no specific goals.

When the researchers re-interviewed the study participants ten years later, the results were shocking.

The 13 percent who had goals but didn't write them down made twice the amount of money as the 84 percent who had reported no goals. But the 3 percent of graduates who had taken time to write out their specific goals were earning *ten times* as much as the other 97 percent of graduates.

Over the years this account has taken on a life of its own because of the power of its message. The biggest—in fact the only—difference between the groups was simply this: clear, written goals.

Becky can attest to the power of written goals and plans. By the time she was twenty-nine years old, she was losing the struggle with time management, finances, procrastination, and the battle of the bulge. The physical, emotional, spiritual, and mental areas of her life were out of control and derailing her relationships and career aspirations.

On a Saturday in February 1984, Becky attended a workshop at a hotel convention center in Chicago. She went in knowing she *needed* to change. She came out knowing *how* to change.

She made a decision on that day to begin a journal, putting her short- and long-term goals in writing and daily tracking and planning her progress in each area of her life. Determined to succeed, Becky gained control over her emotions, got herself into shape, and even produced fitness videos. She began writing books and launched into a nationwide speaking career. And she founded a multimedia company called Becky Tirabassi Change Your Life ®, Inc., that equips people with the resources they need to live better lives.

Having struggled with alcoholism and anger, she knows the difficulty of overcoming character flaws. In her book *Keep the Change*, she encourages readers who truly desire to triumph over their difficulties and bounce back after setbacks to daily record their progress and honestly review their goals. In addition, they must be willing to have accountability partners (coaches, sponsors, counselors, etc.) to help them succeed.

An effective green-to-tee strategy for your life must include a written plan that defines your long-term goals and then divides them into daily steps, manageable increments, and smaller deadlines. As the familiar maxim goes, If you fail to plan, you plan to fail.

My first rule is, "Distance without direction is worse than no distance at all."

NANCY LOPEZ

FUNDAMENTAL #5

Focus on
the Shot

STRIVE ON EVERY SHOT TO MOVE THE CLUB BACK
AS DELIBERATELY AS POSSIBLE, CONSISTENT WITH
SWINGING IT [BACK], RATHER THAN TAKING IT [BACK].

Jack Nicklaus

43

FUNDAMENTAL #5

FOCUS ON THE SHOT

Once a green-to-tee strategy is developed, concentrating on the shot at hand is the best way to achieve maximum performance in golf.

The theory behind this fundamental is that your body performs more effectively and efficiently when your eyes have a specific goal or target. The minute we lose focus, it's almost guaranteed that we won't execute the desired shot. Instead, we'll worry about our score, concentrate on the hazards, consider the odds against us, and compare ourselves with our opponent . . . we'll do everything but get the job done.

Bob Rotella gives this advice: "Eighty percent of any golf shot happens before the player takes the club back: when he aims, takes his grip, addresses the ball, and most important, focuses his mind." It's all about harnessing your mind to focus only on this one shot. It takes

46

FOCUSING ON JUST ONE SHOT REQUIRES THAT YOU FORGET WHAT HAPPENED ON THE LAST HOLE OR EVEN THE PREVIOUS SHOT.

great discipline, but it pays off immeasurably. This is not a fundamental that only the pros can master—all players can train themselves to focus only on the shot in front of them.

Focusing on just one shot requires that you forget what happened on the last hole or even the previous shot. It also keeps you from getting ahead of yourself. Harvey Penick embraces this fundamental in his *Little Red Book*: "Shut out all thoughts other than picking out a target and taking dead aim at it."

FOCUS ON THE SHOT

Though it sounds cliché, no one ever possessed a week, a month, a year, or a decade of change without acquiring it one day at a time. This simple philosophy of life will help both the achiever and the struggler accomplish their goals. The secret is staying focused!

Whether you want to break a bad habit or develop a new one, it will take incredible concentration. Keeping your mind attentive to the task at hand is the defining action that will keep you from getting distracted or giving up.

It seems like it should be easy, but staying focused on a single project, conversation, problem, or task often requires mental toughness

—shutting out all other thoughts and distractions. It means you cannot allow yourself to dwell on the vast distance standing between you and your goals. Neither can you keep looking back, regretting and fretting over the past.

You will have to develop moment-by-moment mental stamina to stay focused. Any thoughts that distract you or cause you to dwell on the negative will hinder you from taking the small, necessary, daily steps that eventually lead you to the fulfillment of your goals. Therefore, be diligent to guard and protect your mind in practical ways.

As mentioned in the previous chapter, we strongly recommend you keep a journal or use another type of written organizer. Look at your day in advance and identify the "shot" you need to make in order to move toward your goal.

Couples who want to focus on improving their relationship could ask and answer three questions every day: Is there something I can do for you today? Is there any way I've hurt you today? Who will keep us accountable to our goals?

A person who wants to improve in physical fitness could address three daily action steps: What healthy foods will I eat at each meal today? How and when will I exercise today? Who will keep me accountable to my goals?

Right now, focus on what you can do *today* to take one step toward your long-term personal or professional goals. Tomorrow, do the same. And the day after, the same . . .

Permanent transformation is attained and sustained in our lives one day at a time.

Hit the shot you know you can hit, not the one you think you should.

BOB ROTELLA

Overcome the Hazards

THE TWO MISTAKES I SEE MOST OFTEN FROM AMATEURS
ARE LIFTING UP AND HITTING THE EQUATOR OF THE
BALL, SENDING IT INTO THE NEXT COUNTY OR TAKING A
DIVOT OF SAND LARGE ENOUGH TO BURY A CAT.

Sam Snead

FUNDAMENTAL #6

OVERCOME THE HAZARDS

The obvious trouble spots on a golf course are water, out-of-bounds markers, deep grass, trees, and bunkers. But the physical obstacles are not a player's only concern. When it comes to navigating the inevitable hazards on any course, players must also overcome any fear attached to executing the shot that will get them out of trouble.

Tom Kite said of his instructor, "Harvey Penick always wanted us to be good bunker players so we wouldn't be afraid to fire at a flag tucked next to one." Greg Norman agrees, suggesting, "Would you like to know the fastest way to take several strokes off your game? Spend two hours in a bunker."

Because every golf course is designed with hazards, it's imperative to know how to overcome them, both emotionally and physically,

53

whether they incur a penalty or not.

How can you do this most effectively?

Before a round, practice a variety of bunker and other difficult shots. During a round, maintain a healthy respect of hazards. Take time on each hole, before teeing off, to identify any trouble spots. A hazard isn't always visible from the tee, so it's wise to view the layout of a hole on the scorecard or ask other players what hazards they know of on the hole. Then design a green-to-tee strategy to avoid the hazards. And on the occasion when you do land in one, calmly consider all of your options before taking the next shot.

It's natural to feel a variety of emotions when you land in a hazard. But minimizing fear or frustration by staying focused and committed to the shot keeps your mind uncluttered and will result in your best physical performance in a difficult situation.

Each golf course is designed to challenge players to overcome its unique hazards, requiring us to be alert, think hard, play smart, and control our emotions.

55

MINIMIZING FRUSTRATION BY STAYING

FOCUSED AND COMMITTED TO THE SHOT

WILL RESULT IN YOUR BEST PHYSICAL

PERFORMANCE IN A DIFFICULT SITUATION.

OVERCOME THE HAZARDS

Life is full of challenges—mistakes for which we're responsible as well as unfortunate setbacks and accidents that are unsolicited, unexpected, or undeserved. In every case, the ability to quickly recover from an injury, insult, or obstruction that knocks the wind out of us is the key to quickly turning negativity in our lives into positive momentum.

A business theory says the determining factor in achieving our goals is the ability to identify and overcome the obstacles. After we identify our dreams and goals, we must write down the specific barriers we'll encounter when attempting to achieve them. For some of us, the barriers, traps, or obstacles will be external (getting financial backing, developing a team, finding a producer or publisher). Others will have internal hazards: negative self-talk, procrastination, addictions, bad time-management, or poor self-image.

After identifying your obstacles, it's necessary to write down a strategy to overcome them. Identify resources, people, and programs to help you conquer these barriers.

For example, as a golfer you might struggle repeatedly with getting

A business theory says the determining factor in achieving our goals is the ability to identify and overcome the obstacles.

out of the sand. You've identified a weakness in your game, now you know where to focus, and maybe you take a series of lessons to improve your bunker play.

Or perhaps you have a fear of public speaking, but you know this skill is necessary if you want to excel in your career. Being aware and admitting you need help in this area is the first step. The action step, taking a class to develop your speaking skills, will not only give you the courage to overcome your fear, but it will provide the opportunity you need to succeed by equipping you with new knowledge and skills that are based on the proven success of others. Incorporating reliable techniques into any aspect of life, business, or relationships will improve your performance.

Another area in which we face obstacles is relationships. In his counseling practice, Roger has found that the top three areas in which couples struggle are finances, parenting, and sexual intimacy.

57

Roger helps them not only to recognize their specific conflicts but also to unemotionally identify the barriers keeping them from achieving their goals.

He does this by giving his clients a conflict-resolution system that helps them develop a practical strategy for overcoming obstacles by brainstorming solutions. Then the couple agrees on a plan of action with specific timelines, regularly evaluating their progress until they achieve their goals.

Rather than letting life's inevitable hazards or difficulties paralyze you, follow these tips:

- Be alert to recurring struggles.
- Brainstorm your options for overcoming each obstacle.
- Ask for help to assess a situation.
- Determine a course of action.
- Evaluate your progress regularly until you succeed.

*Bunkers are not placed on a course haphazard,
but they are made at particular places
to catch particular kinds of defective shots.*

JAMES BRAID

Build Confidence
with Routine

HAVE NO SWING THOUGHTS WHATSOEVER FROM
120 YARDS AND IN. THINK ONLY OF THE TARGET.

Bob Rotella

FUNDAMENTAL #7

BUILD CONFIDENCE WITH ROUTINE

In his book *Golf Is Not a Game of Perfect*, Bob Rotella writes often and passionately about the importance of a pre-shot routine. He says, "A sound pre-shot routine is the rod and staff of the golfer under pressure, a comfort in times of affliction and challenge. It ensures that he gets set up properly, physically and mentally. It blocks out distractions. It helps him to produce his best golf under pressure."

A pre-shot routine (1) removes distracting elements and negative thoughts, (2) narrows one's focus to the shot at hand, and (3) serves to align the body to the target. The result? Improved performance.

Professional golfers use pre-shot routines to put themselves in a groove or zone to swing consistently, especially when emotions or extraneous circumstances threaten their performance. Routine puts

64

ROUTINE
PUTS
PLAYERS
IN A COM-
FORTABLE
MENTAL
STATE,
ENABLING
THEM TO
PERFORM
AT THEIR
PEAK, TIME
AFTER
TIME.

players in a comfortable mental state, enabling them to perform at their peak, time after time.

Our PGA instructor, Rick Hunter, encourages pre-shot routines for golfers at any skill level. He suggests a routine that is simple and personalized based on a systematic sequence of thoughts, check-points, and movements that are executed prior to hitting golf shots.

Though everyone's pre-shot routine will be unique, it should include these basic components:

- A fundamentally sound grip
- Basic athletic posture
- Proper body alignment
- Mental target awareness
- Confident, positive attitude

If you don't currently follow a pre-shot routine but want to have a more confident and consistent swing, contact your local golf professional to help you personalize a routine for your game.

BUILD CONFIDENCE WITH ROUTINE

A daily routine in life has the same effect as a pre-shot routine in golf—it improves your overall performance. In order to reach our maximum potential in the physical, relational, or occupational areas of our lives, we need to develop a daily routine. Just as a pre-shot routine in golf removes distracting elements, a daily written action plan keeps us on track to accomplish the day's planned tasks.

Becky developed a daily routine based on eight action steps that balance all areas of her life—especially when deadlines, stress, or interruptions occur.

In about twenty minutes a day, she can set her body, mind, and spirit for peak performance by following this routine. It's a discipline that requires her to stick with it—not just when she feels like it or if there's time or when it is convenient.

Her routine, found in the *Change Your Life Daily Journal*, includes these four things:

- Eating right—planning a healthy breakfast, lunch, dinner and snacks.

A daily routine
in life has the same effect
as a pre-shot routine in golf—
it improves your
overall performance.

- Exercising regularly—a thirty- to sixty-minute physical activity at least three times a week.
- Detailing her day—using a calendar that has room to list and check off every "To Do" item for that day.
- Defining her dream—on a daily basis, recording short-term goals that help her reach long-term goals.

Keeping a daily journal for more than twenty years has helped Becky control her weight and temperament, truly improve her relationships, grow spiritually, and fulfill many of her dreams as a communicator.

As you picture your pre-shot routine on the golf course, think about what it's intended to do: it sets you up; it brings your mind into focus and your body into alignment. Your daily routine in life serves the same purpose. It helps you step into the day with a battle plan. Creating a daily system that works for you will help you assess your situation and line up your schedule, priorities, and goals. A serious golfer would never haphazardly walk up to the ball and take a careless swing. Why, then, would you step up to your day without diligent preparation that sets you up for success?

If you're struggling to develop a daily routine that helps you complete tasks, keep commitments, and achieve your physical, emotional, and spiritual goals, consider meeting with a life coach, mentor, or counselor to help you develop this important discipline.

Stay Calm, Play Calm

HEAD-LIFTING IS CAUSED BY FEAR AND ANXIETY.
YOU ARE SEEKING THE RESULT BEFORE YOU HAVE
STRUCK THE BALL. YOU DID NOT TRUST YOUR SWING.

Ernest Jones

FUNDAMENTAL #8

STAY CALM, PLAY CALM

Golf is a sport designed to put players in challenging situations, testing their emotional and mental strength as well as their physical and athletic skill.

For example, Pinehurst Country Club in North Carolina is a championship course designed by Donald Ross and known for its crowned, or domed, greens. Their rounded shape leaves little room for error in a golfer's approach shot to the hole. In fact, Pinehurst has a reputation for eliciting fear before a golfer even arrives at the course. It's also known for inspiring outbursts of anger.

But uncontrolled emotion on the course not only derails your game; it can also negatively affect your fellow players.

We recently paired with a fellow whose anger escalated with

74

UNCONTROLLED EMOTION ON THE COURSE NOT ONLY DERAILS YOUR GAME, IT CAN ALSO NEGATIVELY AFFECT YOUR FELLOW PLAYERS.

every hole. By the fourteenth hole, after a bad pitch shot, he let loose and broke his club over his knee. But that wasn't the end of the blowout. Two more clubs, one on each of the next two holes, were snapped in half before the outburst came to an end.

If that wasn't enough drama, his partner finally lost his own temper while taking him to task for such inappropriate behavior.

While all of this was unfolding, Becky was trying to secure her best round of the entire summer. Though she tried to ignore the craziness on the previous two holes, she double bogeyed each, missing her all-time low score by one stroke. Nobody left happy.

Golf requires you to stay calm and play calm, not just so *you* can reach your maximum performance, but so your fellow players can enjoy the game as well.

STAY CALM, PLAY CALM

Are you aware that your thoughts and emotions control your brain's chemistry, which influences your behavior, which affects the lives of those around you?

In his book *Change Your Brain, Change Your Life*, Dr. Daniel Amen contends that negative thinking must be controlled if you

Keeping your cool even enhances your mental capacity and increases your logical thought process.

want to exhibit patience instead of impulsivity, peace instead of anxiety, and faith instead of fear.

Dr. Amen is an expert in the field of helping people plagued by procrastination, addiction, anxiety, or anger. He contends that there are very practical methods for reigning in out-of-control emotions or negative thoughts. He explains how simple deep-breathing techniques can lower your heart rate and create a sense of calm. He also discusses negative thinking at length, giving a name to thoughts that attempt to steal our peace: ANTs (automatic negative thoughts).

Perhaps the key factor in controlling your emotions is patience. Those of us who struggle with addiction, anxiety, or anger have to learn the art of patience—the ability to exhibit an even-temper and self-control in all situations.

People who can stay calm during stress and difficulty are the same people who experience true joy in success yet are gracious in failure, learning from both.

At work, with your family members, as a competitor, or as a customer, staying calm might look like this:

- Listening before speaking
- Waiting twenty-four hours before confronting someone
- Writing out or role-playing a conversation before speaking
- Speaking the truth in love
- Lowering your tone of voice
- Following a proven conflict-resolution system

Controlling your emotions can actually increase your body's physical performance by causing it to relax instead of tighten, leading to peak performance levels rather than constricted or impulsive movement.

Keeping your cool even enhances your mental capacity and increases your logical thought process. Need proof? Think of the last time you tried to make a rational decision while feeling overwhelmed with emotions like anger, fear, or grief.

It isn't easy for most of us, but staying calm *will* positively change every area (and perhaps every relationship) in your life for the better.

Don't let the bad shots get to you. Don't let yourself become angry.
The true scramblers are thick-skinned.
And they always beat the whiners.

PAUL RUNYAN

FUNDAMENTAL #9

Never
Stop
Believing

IN GOLF, WHILE THERE IS LIFE THERE IS HOPE.

Sir Walter Simpson

81

FUNDAMENTAL #9

NEVER STOP BELIEVING

No one will soon forget the Ryder Cup Tournament at Brookline in 1999.

The American roster that year was comprised of some of golf's biggest superstars: Tiger Woods, Phil Mickelson, Payne Stewart, and Davis Love III were among the men following the lead of their captain, Ben Crenshaw. Expectations were high for this team to recapture the Ryder Cup from the Europeans, but the first two days of play gave every indication that the Americans were going to lose.

The U.S. trailed 6–10 heading into the final day of competition. By most accounts, the tournament was over—in fact, no team in the Ryder Cup had ever come back to win from that far behind. They had history, odds, and momentum all working against them.

In his article "Inside Golf's Greatest Comeback," *Golf Digest* writer John Hawkins wrote, "Come Saturday night, the deficit facing Crenshaw's troops appeared insurmountable."

Nevertheless, the U.S. team gathered for one last meeting on the eve of Sunday's finals. The men and their wives walked into the meeting exhausted with the heaviness of certain defeat. But a highly emotional speech by their coach, Ben Crenshaw, was followed by a series of motivational videos, a guest speaker, and then impassioned remarks from each member of the U.S. team. Hope grew, at first slowly—then with rapid momentum—convincing them that the impossible was within their reach.

Without golf clubs in their hands, they knew they first had to believe it was possible to win—and most importantly, they had to never stop believing.

The final day was packed with drama, culminating on the seventeenth hole of the Justin Leonard match. He faced a sixty-foot putt that could give the U.S. team a win. Difficult for any player to make, the putt was watched by millions of viewers worldwide. With exact speed and distance control, the ball rolled perfectly toward the hole. The air seemed electrified as the ball sank into

If you can convince yourself that now is the moment to win,
nothing can stop you.

GARY PLAYER

- When you find yourself in trouble, faith equips you to overcome the hazard and get back on course.
- When you're distracted and disorganized, faith settles you into a routine that builds your confidence.
- When you're overwhelmed by anger, fear, or anxiety, faith calmly restores your peace and joy.

Faith is the final factor in breaking through to permanent transformation. *Whatever* you long to change, faith will empower you to never stop believing in the impossible.